W9-CFQ-282

NEW YORK CITY

FRANK WALSH

WORLD ALMANAC® LIBRARY

Please visit our web site at: www.worldalmanaclibrary.com
For a free color catalog describing World Almanac® Library's list of high-quality books
and multimedia programs, call 1-800-848-2928 (USA) or 1-800-387-3178 (Canada).
World Almanac® Library's fax: (414) 332-3567.

Library of Congress Cataloging-in-Publication Data

Walsh, Frank.
    New York City / by Frank Walsh.
        p. cm. — (Great cities of the world)
    Includes bibliographical references and index.
    ISBN 0-8368-5025-4 (lib. bdg.)
    ISBN 0-8368-5185-4 (softcover)
    1. New York (N.Y.)—Juvenile literature. [1. New York (N.Y.)] I. Title. II. Series.
F128.33.W3   2003
974.7'1—dc21   2003052523

First published in 2004 by
World Almanac® Library
330 West Olive Street, Suite 100
Milwaukee, WI 53212 USA

Copyright © 2004 by World Almanac® Library.

Produced by Discovery Books
Editor: Gianna Williams
Series designers: Laurie Shock, Keith Williams
Designer and page production: Keith Williams
Photo researcher: Rachel Tisdale
Maps and diagrams: Keith Williams
World Almanac® Library editorial direction: Jenette Donovan Guntly
World Almanac® Library editor: Jonny Brown
World Almanac® Library art direction: Tammy Gruenewald
World Almanac® Library production: Beth Meinholz

Photo credits: AKG London: pp.7, 8, 9, 10; AKG London/H. Bock: p.24; AKG London/Keith Collie: pp.5, 25; Art Directors
& Trip/E. Knight: p.38; Art Directors & Trip/H. Rogers: p.16; Art Directors & Trip/J. Braund: p.23; Art Directors & Trip/J.
Cherfas: p.19; Art Directors & Trip/M. Barlow: pp.33, 41; Art Directors & Trip/M. Lee: p.32; Art Directors & Trip/O. Cassill:
p.4; Art Directors & Trip/P. Treanor: cover, title page; Art Directors & Trip/S. Grant: pp.22, 39; Art Directors & Trip/Viesti
Collection: p.42; Corbis/David H.Wells: p.27; Corbis/Duomo: p.36; Corbis/Lynn Goldsmith: p.35; David Simson: pp.14, 28,
34; Hutchison Library/Jeremy Horner: p.29, 31; National Park Service, U.S. Department of the Interior: p.13; Panos
Pictures/Chris Stowers: p.18; Still Pictures/Hartmut Schwarzbach: p.30; Still Pictures/Jeff Greenberg: p.20

Cover caption: Times Square comes alive at night.

Printed in the United States of America

1 2 3 4 5 6 7 8 9 07 06 05 04 03

Contents

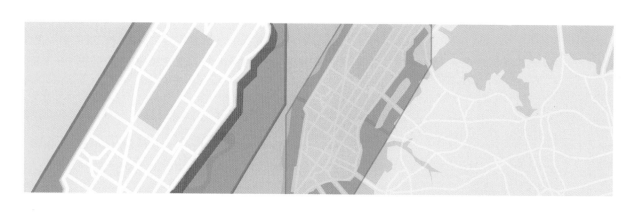

Introduction

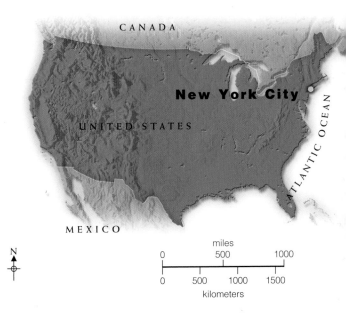

CANADA

New York City

UNITED STATES

ATLANTIC OCEAN

MEXICO

N

miles
0   500   1000
0   500   1000   1500
kilometers

"New York was no mere city. It was instead an infinitely romantic notion, the mysterious nexus of all love and money and power, the shining and perishable dream itself."

—Joan Didion, essayist, 1967.

New York City is, perhaps more than anything else, a city of possibilities and choices. What to do, where to go, what to eat—these are all questions that no city can answer quite as excitingly as New York.

◄ *The New York skyline from the East River. The view shows midtown Manhattan, the Empire State Building lit up by the rising sun.*

The Heart of the United States

New York City is not the capital of New York State. That honor belongs to the city of Albany, about 150 miles (241 kilometers) north of New York City. New York City was briefly the capital of the United States, until the capital was moved to Philadelphia, Pennsylvania. In many ways, though, New York City has always been the true heart of the United States. With a population a little over eight million, New York is the largest city in the country and one the largest cities in the world.

Humble Beginnings

New York City had humble beginnings as a tiny seventeenth-century Dutch settlement. It was always unique though, in that New York is one of the world's finest natural ports. From the island of Manhattan, boats could travel the Hudson River, the Atlantic Ocean, and, later, the Erie Canal. With this geographic advantage, New York became a major trading port, fueling the city's growth.

In many ways, New York City is the ultimate realization of New York state's motto, "Excelsior," a Latin word meaning "ever upward." "Ever upward" is a good description for New York's famous skyline of tall, graceful buildings that seem to reach the sky.

▶ *A winter view of Central Park, facing southeast. Designed in 1856, the park contains the popular Wollman Skating Rink.*

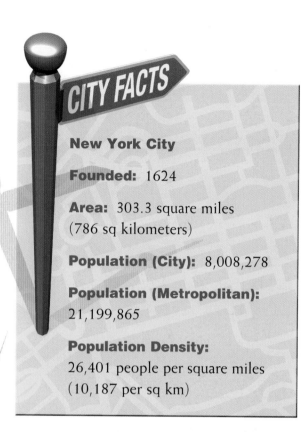

CITY FACTS

New York City

Founded: 1624

Area: 303.3 square miles (786 sq kilometers)

Population (City): 8,008,278

Population (Metropolitan): 21,199,865

Population Density: 26,401 people per square miles (10,187 per sq km)

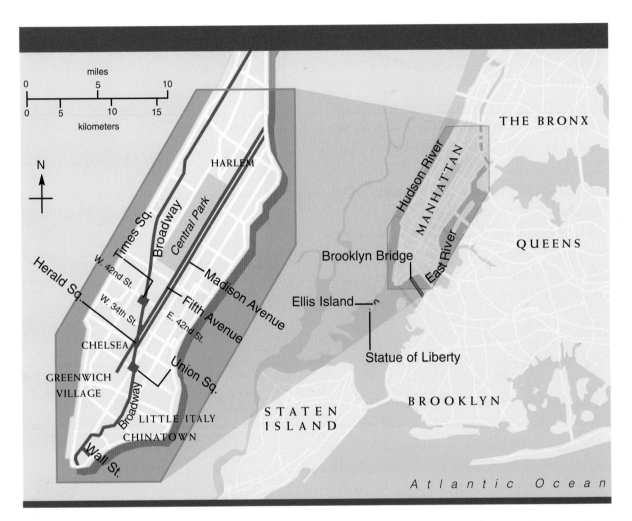

Five Boroughs

When people talk about New York, they are usually referring to Manhattan, an island of parks, buildings, and row after row of streets. Manhattan streets are mostly laid out in a convenient grid pattern, a design that has been in place since the eighteenth century.

There is a lot more to New York City than just Manhattan, though. Manhattan is only one of five different boroughs, or towns, that make up New York City. Each New York City borough is unique.

To the east of Manhattan lies another, much larger island called Long Island. On the western tip of Long Island are two New York City boroughs: Brooklyn and Queens. Brooklyn is the home of both the Brooklyn Museum of Art and Coney Island. Queens was the site of both the 1939 and 1964 World's Fairs.

Southwest of Manhattan is Staten Island, another borough of New York City. Staten Island is famous for Historic Richmond Town, a restored colonial village.

Finally, just to the northeast of Manhattan, there is the Bronx. The Bronx boasts several interesting places to visit, including the Bronx Zoo, the New York Botanical Garden, and Yankee Stadium. The Bronx is actually the only borough of New York City to be connected to New York State. The other four boroughs are all located on islands, or are islands themselves.

Uptown, Midtown, and Downtown

Manhattan is a long, thin vertical rectangle divided into three sections. From the north of the island to just south of Central Park is uptown. The remaining portion of the island can be split into two equal sections: the northern section is midtown, and the southern section is downtown.

Within each of these sections are a number of different neighborhoods. For instance, uptown includes Inwood Heights, Harlem, and two communities on either side of Central Park: the Upper West Side and the Upper East Side.

Midtown, meanwhile, is the entertainment center of the city, and includes the Theater District, the shining lights of Times Square, and the fashion-conscious Garment District.

Downtown is, in many ways, the busiest section of all. Downtown Manhattan includes several neighborhoods: the Financial District, Chinatown, SoHo, Little Italy, the Lower East Side, Greenwich Village, the East Village, Tribeca, Gramercy Park, and Chelsea.

The Brooklyn Bridge

Connecting all of the boroughs of New York City are a series of bridges and tunnels. The most famous of these is the Brooklyn Bridge (on the left), designed by John Roebling. Work on the bridge began in 1869 and continued until 1883. Sadly, Roebling died before the bridge was completed. When the 1,595-foot (486-meter) long bridge opened, it was the longest suspension bridge in the world.

CHAPTER 1

History of New York City

Human beings did not arrive in the New York state area until about 11,000 years ago. The Native Americans who settled in the New York City area were members of the Algonquin nation. They referred to their home as "Manahatta," meaning "hilly island."

First Europeans

The first European to arrive in New York was Giovanni da Verrazano, an Italian who sailed into New York Bay in 1524. He was followed in 1609 by Henry Hudson, an English explorer who worked for a Dutch company. Hudson and his crew arrived in 1609 while trying to discover a new route to Asia. Hudson wrote to his Dutch employers, describing the beauty of the area, the vast amounts of potential farmland, and, most importantly, the abundance of wildlife. At that time, animal skins could be sold for a great profit in Europe.

In order to establish a permanent colony in the area, the Dutch West India Company sent thirty families to Manhattan in 1624. They named their settlement New Amsterdam. Peter Minuit, the first governor of the colony, purchased Manhattan from the

◄ Henry Hudson landed on the site of New York City in 1609. The Hudson River was named for him.

t' Fort nieuw Amsterdam op de Manhatans

Indians for an assortment of knives and trinkets worth roughly $24.

Relations with the Native Americans were turbulent. As the colony grew, the local Indian tribes eventually were forced out. Many Native Americans died because they had no immunity to the foreign diseases, like smallpox and the measles, which the Europeans accidentally brought over with them.

British or Dutch?
The colony of New Amsterdam continued to grow steadily, eventually spreading out into the neighboring areas of Long Island and Staten Island. The success of the colony, though, came to the attention of the British. At the time, the British and Dutch empires were fierce rivals and were both greedy for territory in the New World.

▲ *An engraving shows the settlement of "New Amsterdam" as it looked in about 1614.*

Charles II, the British king, granted his brother James, the Duke of York, the right to the land claimed by the Dutch. The duke immediately sent warships to New Amsterdam. On September 8, 1664, the colony surrendered to the British and was renamed New York in honor of the duke.

"The land is excellent and agreeable, full of noble forest trees and grape vines, and nothing is wanting but the labor and industry of man to render it one of the finest and most fruitful lands in that part of the world…"

—Johan de Laet, author and explorer, 1625.

Revolution and Destruction

Ironically, it was because of the success of ports like New York that relations between the British and the American colonists began to sour in the middle of the eighteenth century.

After 1763, when Britain won control of much of North America in the French and Indian War, the British government began to impose severe trade laws on the colonists. The outrage many colonists felt over these laws was compounded when the British began to tax goods like paper, glass, and tea.

In 1775, war broke out between the Americans and their colonial masters. The following year, General William

▲ This color lithograph of Lower Broadway was made around 1834. The settlement of the city began at the south end of Broadway, near Battery Park.

Howe and 20,000 British troops captured New York City. During the British occupation a series of explosions and fires caused tremendous damage to the city. It is possible that these fires were in fact set by New Yorkers who were prepared to see their city destroyed rather than let it fall into the hands of the British. The British evacuated New York in 1783, leaving the city in ruins. New Yorkers quickly set about rebuilding and restoring their city as a center of trade and business.

A New Country's Capital

In 1785, New York became the temporary capital of the United States of America. It was there that George Washington was sworn in as the nation's first president in 1789. In 1790, however, the capital was temporarily moved from New York to Philadelphia as northerners and southerners argued over the best place for its permanent location. The two groups finally settled on a tract of land along the banks of the Potomac River. That site was developed into Washington, D.C., and the naton's capital was permanently moved there in 1800.

Expansion and Civil War

In the nineteenth century, advances in sailing, coupled with the opening of the Erie Canal in 1825, continued to fuel New York's growth into one of the world's major ports. Such prosperity was marred slightly by the Civil War (1861–1865). Although no fighting took place in New York, the draft law passed in March 1863 triggered a week-long series of riots in July of that year. The

"'Go ahead' is our maxim and password; and we do go ahead with a vengeance, regardless of consequences and indifferent about the value of human life."

—Philip Hone, Mayor of New York, 1837.

The Erie Canal

The Erie Canal stretches from Lake Erie to the Hudson River near Albany. Opened in 1825, the 363-mile (584-km) long canal was built to open up the West and Midwest to trade and shipping. Until the arrival of the railroads in the middle of the nineteenth century, the Erie Canal was one of the most convenient routes west. Today, what is left of the canal is used mainly for recreation.

riots were started by white, working-class New Yorkers who resented the idea of risking their lives to free southern slaves. Rich New Yorkers were often excused from the draft, so class resentment also played a part in the riots.

Shaping the City

Until 1898, the term New York City referred only to Manhattan Island. In that year, however, city leaders pushed for the five boroughs—Brooklyn, Queens, Staten Island, the Bronx, and Manhattan—to be combined into the City of Greater New York. This plan was put forward by wealthy New Yorkers, who wanted to establish New York as one of the world's largest cities. Some, like the proud residents of Brooklyn, resisted this change, but the consolidation of the boroughs went ahead, raising the combined population of New York to 3.35 million.

City of Immigrants

During the nineteenth and early twentieth centuries, New York City's population soared. The main reason for the rise was immigration. Immigrants flooded into New York, providing the city with an abundance of cheap labor. They raised buildings, worked on the docks, manufactured goods, and constructed the bridges and subways that are still used today. After 1886 immigrants sailing into New York's harbor were greeted by the Statue of Liberty, a gift to the United States from France.

African American Migration

Not all of New York City's new residents came from foreign countries. In fact, many were from other parts of the United States. New York state outlawed slavery in 1827, almost forty years before the Thirteenth Amendment freed all slaves. Because New York City was in a "free" state, it was attractive to many African Americans at the time. Decades later, after World War I ended in 1918, thousands of southern African Americans moved north, looking for work in industrialized cities. Many moved to the area just north of Central Park known as Harlem. In the 1920s that area

"Give me your tired, your poor, your huddled masses yearning to breathe free..."

—Inscription on the Statue of Liberty
by Emma Lazarus, 1883.

experienced a period often known as the Harlem Renaissance, when African-American arts and culture flourished.

The prosperity of the 1920s ended with the collapse of the stock market in the Wall Street Crash in 1929, followed by the Great Depression. Despite valiant efforts to improve standards of living by Fiorello LaGuardia, the mayor of New York during the 1930s and 1940s, the city did not fully recover from the Depression until after World War II.

Limiting Immigration

Fear of unemployment and racial tensions fueled anti-immigration legislation in the early twentieth century. After World War I, American public opinion reacted against all things foreign. Feelings were particularly strong against Asian immigrants, as well as Central and South European immigrants. Quotas on immigrants from each country were set in 1921 by the National Origins Act. The Johnson-Reed Act of 1924 further limited the number of immigrants coming into the country. By mid-century, many of New York's ethnic neighborhoods had begun to shrink.

All this changed in 1965, when immigration quotas were relaxed. Once again, hundreds of thousands of immigrants went to New York. The new immigrants included Latinos, Jamaicans, Guyanese, Ecuadorians, and Haitians, as well as many Eastern and Southeastern Asians.

Ellis Island

Compared to Manhattan, Long Island, and Staten Island, Ellis Island is very small. In terms of history, though, Ellis Island is of tremendous importance. It was here that a station for processing immigrants was built (above). *From 1892 until 1954, more than 16 million immigrants passed through Ellis Island. Today Ellis Island is a museum.*

Rise and Decline of Shipping

New York City's fortunes were built on the shipping industry. At one time, massive ocean liners like the *Queen Mary* were the most popular form of world travel, and New York was a popular destination for rich Europeans.

During World War II, nearly one-third of the troops who went to fight overseas sailed from New York City. The Brooklyn Navy Yard was where many warships were either built or repaired.

In the 1950s, though, the New York City shipping industry went into decline, partly due to containerization, a new method of shipping goods which required less labor. Passenger ships began to lose customers with the growth of commercial air travel.

Tough Times

In the second half of the twentieth century, New York experienced more economic difficulties. It nearly went bankrupt in 1975 and suffered another crash on Wall Street in 1987. In the 1990s Mayor Rudolph Giuliani became world famous for his successful efforts to reduce crime and improve the city's economy and quality of life.

Economic and social difficulties, however, were small compared to the shock of September 11, 2001, when Islamic terrorists destroyed the twin towers of the World Trade Center, killing thousands of people, and altering the city's skyline—and world politics—forever.

CHAPTER 2

People of New York City

New York City is, by any definition, a crowded place. The population density is about 26,400 people per square mile (10,200 per sq km). In comparison, the population density of most cities in the United States is only about 3,000 per sq mi. Oklahoma City, a much smaller urban area, has only about 834 people per square mile (321 per sq km).

New York City is the largest city in the United States, and the population continues to grow. Between 1990 and 2000, the population of New York City grew by 9.4 percent, to an all-time peak of over eight million people. Different areas grow at different rates. From 1990 to 2000, the number of people living in Queens grew by 14.2 percent, while the population of Staten Island grew by 17.1 percent.

The most heavily populated borough of New York City is Brooklyn, where 31 percent of New Yorkers live. Next comes Queens, with 28 percent of the population. Nineteen percent of New Yorkers live in Manhattan, while 16.5 percent live in the Bronx. Staten Island is the smallest borough, with only 5.5 percent of the city's population living there.

◀ *Since its beginnings, New York has welcomed people from many countries and cultures.*

Today's Immigrants

Immigration has played a crucial part in the increase in population. In the 1980s there was a 104 percent increase in New York City's Asian population. Some were Chinese, but many were Korean and Vietnamese immigrants. In the 1990s nearly 1.2 million new immigrants arrived in New York City. By 2000, more than one-third of New York City's total population was foreign-born. This has more than made up for the fact that many longstanding residents of the city are moving to other parts of the nation. The immigrants arriving in New York are also generally younger than existing residents, and therefore tend to have more children, fueling the current population growth.

Poverty

Despite the huge wealth that circulates in New York City, many of its citizens live in poverty. As much as 21.2 percent of the population lives below the poverty line. Among children under five, 29.8 percent live in poverty, as do 29 percent of twelve- to seventeen-year-olds, an age group particularly vulnerable to the destructive influences of crime and drugs. Poverty levels vary from one borough to another.

"No other American city is so intensely American as New York."

—Anthony Trollope, British author, 1862.

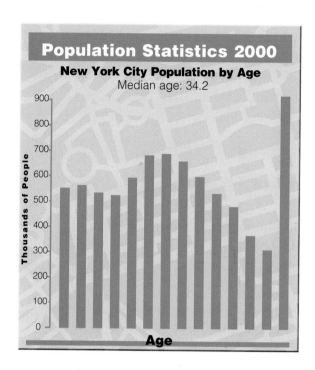

Population Statistics 2000

New York City Population by Age
Median age: 34.2

Poverty by Age 2000

New York City Residents Below Poverty Level by Age
21.2% of total population

- 75 and over **4.5%**
- 65 to 74 **5.1%**
- 45 to 64 **16%**
- Under 5 **9.2%**
- 5 to 11 **14.7%**
- 12 to 17 **10.4%**
- 18 to 44 **40.1%**

▲ *Almost a quarter of the population of New York City lives in poverty, and almost 10 percent of those are under five years of age.*

The Bronx is the poorest borough in New York City: 30.7 percent of the population lives under the poverty line, rising to 43.1 percent among five to eleven-year-old children. In contrast the richest borough in New York is Queens, where just 14.5 percent of the population is below the poverty line.

Ethnic Communities

At one time, it was thought that all the different immigrant populations coming to

▼ *Located in lower Manhattan, the district of Chinatown adjoins City Hall, the city's courts, and the Wall Street area.*

the city would shed their differences and become one uniform group, creating a "Melting Pot" of people. Thankfully, this hasn't happened. Instead, New York City's people retain their individual differences.

Relationships among all these people, with their wildly different backgrounds and customs, haven't always been easy. Occasionally, racial tensions erupt into violence. At different times in New York history, riots have occurred, many of them sparked by conflicts between members of different ethnic groups.

In recent decades, particular groups have made a big impact on the culture and social

fabric of New York City. Most notable of these groups are the Hispanics and African Americans, who together make up a sizeable portion of the city's population.

Hispanics

Hispanics make up just over one quarter of the population of New York City. Most of them are from Puerto Rico, but some have come from Cuba, the Dominican Republic, Central America, and South America. At first, Hispanics settled in southeast Harlem, which has long been called Spanish Harlem. Today the Hispanic population is more evenly spread throughout the city.

Spanish could be called New York City's unofficial second language. Approximately 25 percent of the people who live in New York City speak Spanish at home. Hispanics have their own Spanish-language newspaper, *El Diario La Prensa*, and many ads on subways and buses are written in both Spanish and English.

African Americans

African Americans make up another quarter of New York's population. Throughout the nineteenth and twentieth centuries, African Americans migrated north to cities like New York, hoping to

▶ *The African American and Hispanic communities are the largest in New York City. When considered together, they are a larger group than the white, non-Hispanic community.*

"In New York alone there are more persons of German descent than persons of native descent, and the German element is larger than in any city of Germany except Berlin. There are nearly twice as many Irish as in Dublin, about as many Jews as in Warsaw, and more Italians than in Naples or Venice."

—Robert Hunter, social worker, 1904.

find work and opportunities. New York City continues to have the largest population of African Americans in the United States.

In New York City, the African-American community has enjoyed growing levels of

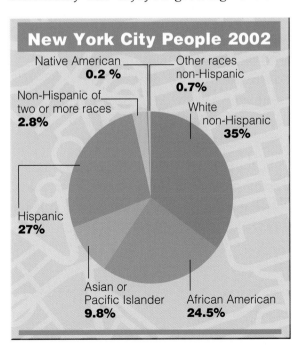

New York City People 2002

Native American **0.2 %**

Other races non-Hispanic **0.7%**

Non-Hispanic of two or more races **2.8%**

White non-Hispanic **35%**

Hispanic **27%**

Asian or Pacific Islander **9.8%**

African American **24.5%**

prosperity in the last few decades. During the 1980s and 1990s, the black middle class grew significantly.

Religious Life

More than 43 percent of New Yorkers are Catholics. This large number is due in part to the waves of immigrants who came to the city from the Catholic countries of Ireland and Italy, as well as to the large Hispanic population. The most famous Catholic Church in New York City is St. Patrick's Cathedral on Fifth Avenue.

The Episcopal Trinity Church on Wall Street has been a city landmark since it was founded in 1697. After the World Trade Center attacks of 2001, however, it became famous as one of the few buildings in the immediate area to survive destruction. Far uptown is another well-known Episcopal church, the Cathedral of St. John the Divine. This cathedral has been under construction since 1892, and when it is completed (likely in 2050) it will be the largest in the world.

Other religions are also practiced in New York City. Jews worship at synagogues like Temple Emanu-El, located on 65th Street. The Emanu-El congregation was founded in 1845 and the synagogue built in 1929. Meanwhile, New York City's Muslims

worship at mosques like the Islamic Cultural Center.

A World of Festivals

New York City's immigrants have shaped the city's festive culture. The Irish, for instance, celebrate St. Patrick's Day every

▶ St. Patrick's Cathedral is situated on Fifth Avenue in midtown. Built in 1880, the cathedral is surrounded by skyscrapers and upscale department stores.

March 17 with a big parade that includes singing, dancing, and banners that proclaim "Erin go Bragh" (an Irish Gaelic phrase meaning "Ireland Forever").

While New York City is famous for the giant Christmas tree that is set up in Rockefeller Center, a large menorah (branched candlestick) is also displayed on Fifth Avenue every year to celebrate the Jewish festival of Hanukkah.

The Chinese New Year falls in January or February, on a different date each year. The celebration takes place primarily in Chinatown. It is a colorful festival, where people dressed up as dragons dance

through the streets while fireworks explode overhead.

Since 1926 the Feast of San Gennaro has been held each September in Little Italy, a section of Manhattan's Lower East Side. This ten-day festival is famous for its variety of delicious foods, including pizza, pasta, and pastries.

New Festivals

Recent immigrants from Latin America, South America, and the Caribbean have brought their festivals with them. The first Puerto Rican Day parade was held in 1958, while Caribbean Americans celebrate Mardi Gras—the Tuesday before Lent— with an annual parade on Brooklyn's Eastern Parkway.

▼ The traditional St. Patrick's Day Parade is held on Fifth Avenue.

CHAPTER 3

Living in New York City

In New York City, there is no real distinction between areas where people can live and where they work. Often buildings will be divided into both offices and apartments. Although there is a great cluster of famous companies between Times Square and the southern tip of Central Park, businesses are located throughout the city, as are people's homes.

Little Cities

Historically, the many immigrants who chose to make their homes in New York City often did so in a particular area. This trend continues even today. The Lower East Side was where many Jews once lived. In recent years, however, the Jewish population has spread out to parts of the Bronx and particularly Brooklyn. Brooklyn is also home to a large Russian population.

Little Italy is located on the Lower East Side. Dozens of Italian restaurants can be found in this neighborhood.

Very near to Little Italy is Chinatown. Chinatown is a fascinating place to visit, with its beautiful temples, Chinese-language bookstores, and telephone booths in the style of pagodas. The population of

◀ Brownstones are row houses peculiar to New York, named for the stone from which they were built.

Greenwich Village

Greenwich Village is a particularly well-known Manhattan neighborhood. "The Village" is located south of 14th Street and west of Washington Square Park. The Village is known for its architecture, which includes several old buildings, and MacDougal Alley. In the twentieth century the area became a home for writers, poets, and musicians. Several jazz clubs like the Village Vanguard and the Blue Note can be found there.

Chinatown has grown so much that new Asian immigrants, including Chinese, have settled away from Manhattan. Many have chosen to live in Brooklyn and Queens.

Many Indian families live in the Jackson Heights section of Queens, but there is also an area in Manhattan on Sixth Street where there is a stretch of fine Indian restaurants.

Rich and Poor

Even though two neighborhoods might be close together, the kinds of people who live in each, and the quality of life for those residents, can be radically different. Harlem is predominantly African American, while the Upper East Side is mostly white. Harlem is generally thought of as a "poor" neighborhood, though it has its share of wealthier homeowners. Many Harlem residents live in modest, sometimes run-down apartments. More affluent residents of the Upper East Side, on the other hand, can afford to live in new or modernized, better mantained, and sometimes much larger spaces. One thing

"Everybody ought to have a Lower East Side in their life."

—Irving Berlin, composer, 1962.

all New York residents have in common, though, is the expense of living in the city. Compared to housing in most other U.S. cities, the housing units in New York tend to be smaller and to cost much more.

Homelessness

On the extreme end, the desperately poor cannot afford to live anywhere and are considered homeless. Current estimates place the number of homeless New Yorkers at around 30,000. Although many of these people find temporary accommodations in one of the city's many homeless shelters,

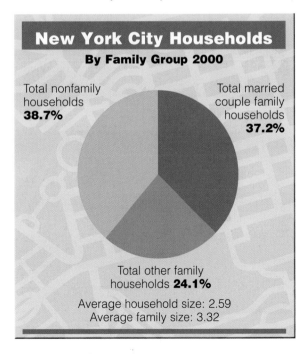

New York City Households
By Family Group 2000

Total nonfamily households **38.7%**

Total married couple family households **37.2%**

Total other family households **24.1%**

Average household size: 2.59
Average family size: 3.32

their lives will not be changed without long-term financial support.

Getting Around

When most Americans think about transportation, they think of cars. In New York, though, there are lots of different ways to travel through the city.

Some New Yorkers do own and drive cars. Very wealthy people can even afford to ride in expensive limousines, which cruise the streets with their tinted windows. However, traffic in New York City is severely congested. With the number of cars in Manhattan traffic at about a million every day, most people rely on taxis or one of the several modes of public transportation.

Cabs and Buses

New York taxis are easy to spot because they are always yellow, and there are a lot of them. It is estimated that there are roughly 12,000 taxis in the city. Taxi driving is a popular occupation for new immigrants to America. Taxis can be expensive though, and many people prefer to take the bus. Buses are less costly and convenient, but both buses and taxis are still victims of traffic gridlock.

Going Underground

Possibly the most efficient way to get around New York City is by going

▼ *"New York's finest," as the police force of New York is fondly known, are constantly checking up on things. Here, an officer asks to see a driver's license.*

▲ *At rush hour, this subway would be packed with people, known as "straphangers." New York's subways run 24 hours a day, seven days a week.*

underground. The city's first underground subway line opened in 1904. Today, the New York subway and elevated train system has 468 stations and almost 700 miles (1,100 km) of track. Although the service can be unpredictable, almost half of all New Yorkers use the subway to get to and from work.

"New York is a city of conversations overheard, of people at the next restaurant table (micrometers away) checking your watch, of people reading the stories in your newspaper on the subway train."

—William E. Geist, author, 1986.

People who live in the outer boroughs of New York have a number of different ways to journey to and from the city. Many subway and bus lines, for example, travel between boroughs. Drivers, on the other hand, can reach the city via underground

Staten Island Ferry

One of the most enjoyable ways to travel into Manhattan is on the Staten Island Ferry. This service, which has been operating since 1905, transports more than 19 million people every year. It takes approximately twenty-five minutes to cover the 5.2-mile (8.3-km) distance from the tip of lower Manhattan to Staten Island. Because the view of lower Manhattan is beautiful and foot passengers ride free, the Staten Island Ferry has become something of a bargain tourist attraction for many visitors to New York.

tunnels, like the Queens-Midtown Tunnel, or bridges, like the Brooklyn Bridge and the Triborough Bridge.

New York City Architecture

New York City has always been known for its architecture. In fact, many buildings there are internationally recognized.

Arguably, the most impressive buildings in New York are the skyscrapers. The word skyscraper implies dizzying heights, but the earliest skyscrapers in New York are quaint by today's standards. The Bayard-Condict Building, erected in 1899, is only thirteen stories high. The Flatiron Building, completed three years later, soars to twenty-one stories, and has a distinctive triangular shape. The age of the modern skyscraper was ushered in with the 77-story Chrysler Building, completed in 1930. The 102-story Empire State Building, considered by many to be the ultimate symbol of New York City, was completed just one year later.

Some of the most beautiful buildings in New York, though, are not necessarily the tallest. Among them are the spiral-shaped Guggenheim Museum, the squat head-quarters

"…at night, when the great walls of masonry are all a-sparkle, the city is fairy-like. It is more beautiful than any other city since the days of the Arabian Nights."

—Mark Twain, author, 1900.

The World Trade Center

Two of the most recent tall additions to the Manhattan skyline were the World Trade Center towers, completed in 1973. Among the world's tallest buildings, both towers were 110 stories tall and reached 1,368 feet (417 meters) into the sky. The "Twin Towers" quickly became symbols of New York's place in the modern world. On September 11, 2001, the New York skyline was altered forever when terrorists destroyed these remarkable towers.

Six months later, on March 11, 2002, two great beams of light shone into the air just north of where the Trade Center towers once stood. For the next thirty-two nights, these lights shone as a memorial to the people who lost their lives on September 11th. A permanent memorial is still being designed.

of the United Nations, and the recently restored Grand Central Terminal. New York also has a number of beautiful cathedrals, like St. Patrick's Cathedral on Fifth Avenue.

Squares

New York City's "squares," such as Times Square, Herald Square, and Union Square, are all found along the curving street known as Broadway. While most of the streets in New York follow the rigid grid pattern, Broadway slices diagonally north to south through Manhattan.

Small parks are characteristic of some of the squares, but not the most famous—Times Square. Instead of grass and trees, Times Square is decorated with billboards and lights. Hundreds of thousands of people gather there every New Year's Eve to count down the seconds to the New Year.

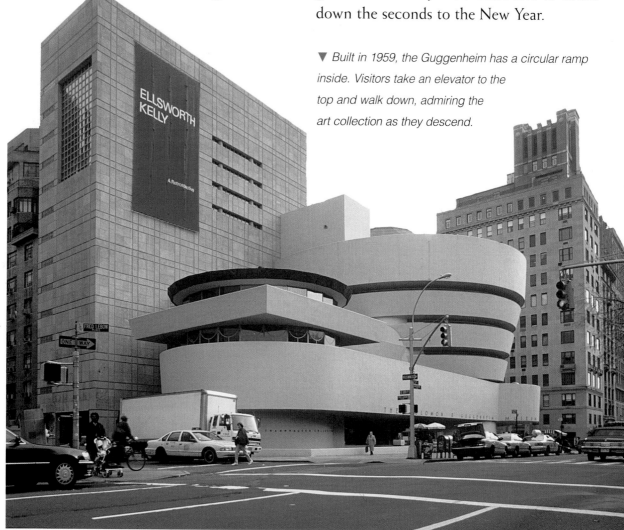

▼ *Built in 1959, the Guggenheim has a circular ramp inside. Visitors take an elevator to the top and walk down, admiring the art collection as they descend.*

Education in New York City

Millions of people attend school in New York City every year—and not all of these students are children.

The public school system in New York is run by the citywide Department of Education. That department oversees the administration of approximately twelve hundred schools. The needs of those schools vary depending on the needs of the children who attend them. Children who do not speak English, for instance, require bilingual education.

Private Education

Not all children in New York City attend public school, though. New York also has a large number of independent, or private, schools. These include the United Nations International School in Manhattan and the Horace Mann School in Riverdale, which is part of the Bronx.

Sometimes, parents send their children to a school that reflects their family's religious beliefs. As a result, there are nearly two hundred Catholic schools in the city. Jewish schools, like the Abraham Joshua Heschel School, are also well attended.

Universities and Colleges

After completing their elementary and high school education, many students choose to continue their studies at one of the many private universities in New York City. These include Columbia University and New York

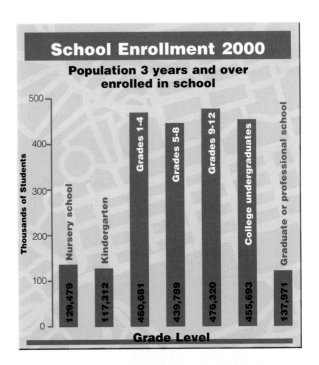

School Enrollment 2000

Population 3 years and over enrolled in school

Thousands of Students — Grade Level

- Nursery school: 129,479
- Kindergarten: 117,312
- Grades 1-4: 460,681
- Grades 5-8: 439,789
- Grades 9-12: 476,320
- College undergraduates: 455,693
- Graduate or professional school: 137,971

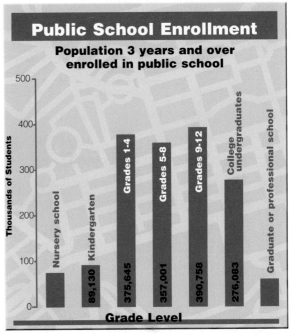

Public School Enrollment

Population 3 years and over enrolled in public school

Thousands of Students — Grade Level

- Nursery school
- Kindergarten: 89,130
- Grades 1-4: 375,645
- Grades 5-8: 357,001
- Grades 9-12: 390,758
- College undergraduates: 276,083
- Graduate or professional school

▲ *Over three-quarters of the city's students attend public school from grades one through twelve.*

▲ Pupils at Bank Street School on New York's Upper West Side surf the Internet.

University. For those who cannot afford the high cost of a private university, there are also schools like the City University of New York, which offers quality education at a much lower cost than most private colleges.

Specialty Schools

Education, though, isn't merely a matter of elementary school, high school, and college. New York also has a number of specialty schools. The Juilliard School, located next to the Lincoln Center for the Performing Arts, is renowned for its music, theater, and dance. The Fashion Institute of Technology is where many important leaders in fashion and design, like Calvin Klein, Barbara Anne Hirsh, and make-up artist Roy Galifi studied. Rockefeller University, meanwhile, is a famous medical research university that includes a hospital.

Many schools cater to adult education, offering classes at night or on weekends when people do not have to work. Perhaps the best known of these is the New School University, which offers classes in acting, music, and design.

American Citizenship

Because of the city's large immigrant population, New York has many schools that teach English as a second language. The ability to speak, read, and write English is a requirement for naturalization, or becoming a citizen of the United States. Another requirement is a firm grasp of the history and government of the United States. Most applicants for citizenship take a test to demonstrate their abilities and knowledge in these areas.

CHAPTER 4

New York City at Work

New York has been described as "the city that never sleeps." While it is a city of around-the-clock activity, as much of this activity is due to work as it is to play.

In New York City, there are almost as many different types of jobs as there are different types of people. Very high-paying jobs include those of some professional athletes, entertainers, lawyers, professionals in banking and finance, and other businesspeople. Most New Yorkers, though, work in jobs that don't receive a lot of attention.

Roughly 20 percent of the New York workforce is made up of office workers. Some of these people are secretaries, billing clerks, and bookkeepers. Ten percent of the workforce is in sales, including the retail staff employed by the large department stores like Macy's and Bloomingdale's. Education is the next biggest sector in the city, employing seven percent of the workforce, and including teachers of different levels and librarians.

New Yorkers also work as barbers, doormen, chefs, and in many other branches of what is called the service industry. A person who works in the service

◄ *"Dig We Must" is the motto of Con Edison, New York City's electricity supplier.*

industry provides a specific service to people. These jobs are taken by more than 20 percent of the workforce. Many of these jobs do not have typical nine to five workdays. For instance, people who are employed to clean office buildings usually start their work day around 6:00 P.M., just after the office workers have gone home. Likewise, hospital workers may be "on call" at any time of the day or night. New York City also has a number of all-night delicatessens and restaurants that have to be staffed.

Unemployment

The unemployed have a hard time in New York because it is such an expensive city. Currently, about 8 percent of New Yorkers who can work are unemployed.

Sometimes, people are unemployed for only a short period. Others cannot find a job because they do not have skills that are

▲ *One of New York's most popular food stores is Zabar's, on Broadway. Zabar's specializes in Jewish delicacies.*

in demand. The chronically unemployed can receive state aid in the form of welfare, but such assistance is often not enough. Those who are unemployed for long periods may join the ranks of the city's homeless.

The Garment Industry

One of New York's most historic industries is the garment industry. The center of the industry is at Seventh Avenue and 34th Street, also known as the Garment District. This is where many companies that make and sell clothing are headquartered. Unlike the shipping industry, the garment industry shows no signs of slowing down, and garment workers are regularly seen pushing racks of clothing through the streets.

The Stock Exchange

At the southern tip of Manhattan is an area of New York City known as the Financial District. The New York Stock Exchange (NYSE), the largest stock exchange in the world, is located there.

The business of stocks is a complicated matter. A share of stock represents a small part of the ownership of a company. Most large businesses sell shares of stock in their company. Investors—people who purchase shares of stock—have a stake in the company and are entitled to a portion of its earnings. A stock exchange is a market where shares of stock can be bought or sold. The transactions that take place in the New York Stock Exchange affect businesses and people all over the world.

The New York Stock Exchange was founded in 1792 by a group of twenty-four traders. In recent years, there have been rumors of the stock exchange moving to New Jersey, but this has not yet happened. Even the terrorist attacks on the World Trade Center towers, which were very near the stock exchange, only closed the NYSE for a total of six days.

A Day on the Stock Exchange

Every weekday from 9:30 A.M. to 4:00 P.M. the stock exchange is a blur of activity. From a gallery that looks down upon the trading floor, people can watch the thousands of brokers, people who buy and sell stocks for others, work on the floor of the exchange.

▲ Stock brokers are busy on the floor of the New York Stock Exchange, in the heart of the financial district.

The brokers buy and sell stocks at one of the seventeen trading posts in the stock exchange. Trading posts are like little stores that buy and sell stock, and each of the trading posts deals with over one hundred stocks. Every post has a number of trading positions, like checkout counters in a grocery store, where the buying and selling of stocks is done.

Banks and Business

The Financial District is also the site of many New York City banks. One particularly important bank is the Federal Reserve Bank of New York. Beneath this building, roughly 80 feet (24 m) below street level, is a vault containing 9,000 tons of gold bars. These bars date back to a time when United States currency was backed by gold, a standard that ended in 1973. Although the gold standard is no longer used to back the value of currency, gold itself is still valuable. The gold supply in the Federal Reserve Bank, a good deal of which is foreign-owned, is estimated at $116 billion.

Apart from stock exchanges and banks, New York is a key city for any major business. Although office space in Manhattan can be extremely expensive, large corporations feel that they need to have a presence there because an office in New York is a sign of real success.

Newspapers and Magazines

Today, people all around the world seem to crave information. New York City, one of

Wall Street

Wall Street (below) got its name from a defensive wall built around the southern tip of the city in 1653. The wall itself has since disappeared, but Wall Street marks the spot where it once stood, reaching from Broadway over to the East River.

the world centers for media, has always been able to provide that information.

Several newspapers with large circulations are written and printed in New York City. The *Daily News* and the *New York Post* are just two examples. Perhaps the most familiar of all New York newspapers, though, is the legendary *New York Times*. First published in 1851, the *Times* is well known for its slogan, "All the news that's fit to print." Also highly regarded is the *Wall Street Journal*, which is read by people interested in the business news.

New York is the home of several free newspapers as well, including the *New York Press* and the *Villager*. Probably the most famous free paper, though, is the weekly *Village Voice*. In print since 1955, the *Voice* offers a more radical take on current events, politics, and the arts.

New York City is also where quite a few magazines are produced. Each edition of the *New Yorker*, *New York Magazine*, *Time*, and *Newsweek* comes out of offices in New York, and is read both nationally and internationally. Book publishing, too, has always been a big business in New York. The employees of many large publishing companies, including Random House, Simon and Schuster, and Viking, conduct their business in Manhattan offices.

▼ *News reporters and television camera crews interview protestors on the steps of City Hall.*

Broadcasting and Film

All of the major television networks have headquarters in Manhattan, the most spectacular of which are the offices of the National Broadcasting Company (NBC) at Rockefeller Center. The evening news programs from NBC, ABC, CBS, and even PBS are all broadcast from New York City. Many New York radio stations, such as 1010 WINS, broadcast news stories twenty-four hours a day.

The movie industry is also very much at home in New York City. Many big-budget movies have been shot there, such as *Annie Hall*, *Do the Right Thing*, *Godzilla*, and *Spiderman* to name just a few. It is not uncommon to see film crews and actors at work in a New York street, shooting the latest blockbuster. New York City's skyline is so famous, and has appeared so often in films and photographs, that there have even been attempts made at copyrighting it.

Madison Avenue

Madison Avenue is the home of modern advertising in the United States. At one time, a number of major advertising agencies had their offices on this Manhattan street. Eventually the term "Madison Avenue" came to refer to the entire industry of advertising. In recent times, advertising agencies have moved to different locations throughout the country. Likewise, many New York City advertising agencies, like J. Walter Thompson, McCann-Erickson, and Ogilvy & Mather, have moved from Madison Avenue to other parts of the city. Young & Rubicam is one of the major agencies that have kept their offices on Madison Avenue.

Running New York City

Running New York City is a complicated task. The city government breaks down into three bodies: the mayor, the Board of Estimate, and the City Council. The City Council introduces and passes local laws ranging from public safety to health and the environment. The Board of Estimate is responsible for city planning and budgeting.

City Council

The City Council comprises fifty-one members from fifty-one different council districts throughout the five boroughs. Council members are elected every four years and represent districts of about 157,000 people each. The council's law-making work is mostly done by committees. Each council member serves on at least three different committees that meet at least once a month. Most council hearings are held twice a month in the Council

Chambers or the adjoining Committee Room in City Hall. The Council Speaker is elected by council members and is responsible for obtaining a consensus on major issues.

FDNY

The Fire Department of New York is responsible for putting out blazes in the 303-square mile (786-sq km) area of New York City. The 15,400 employees of the FDNY consist of 11,400 fire officers and fire fighters, 2,800 emergency medical technicians, and roughly 1,200 civilian employees. On September 11, 2001, 343 members of the FDNY lost their lives attempting to save others during the terrorist attacks.

▲ *Former Mayor Rudolph Giuliani and his then-wife, Donna Hanover, are interviewed by the media.*

Mayor and Council

It is the mayor, however, who is the true face of the city. The mayor can choose to sign or veto bills that have been passed by the council. If he or she signs the bill, it immediately becomes a local law. If the mayor vetoes a bill, it is returned to the City Council with the mayor's objections. The Council has thirty days to override the mayor's veto. If the council passes the bill again by a vote of two-thirds (at least thirty-four members in favor), it is then considered adopted and becomes law.

Famous Mayors

Over the years, New York has had many "celebrity mayors." Perhaps the first of these was Fiorello LaGuardia. In office from 1934 to 1945. LaGuardia is remembered as a warm, funny man who read comic strips over the radio during a newspaper strike. Edward Koch, who served from 1978 to 1989, was known for his catchphrase, "How am I doing?" Rudolph Giuliani, the mayor of New York at the turn of the present century, was already world-famous for his efforts at tackling crime in the city when he became internationally renowned for his actions after the terrorist attacks of September 11, 2001, on the World Trade Center.

CHAPTER 5

New York City at Play

Whether people are interested in exercising their minds or their muscles, there are plenty of ways to do both in New York City.

Broadway and Beyond

The first play was performed in New York City in 1732. Since then, New York has become one of the great theater cities of the world. Thirty-eight different theaters are crammed into the Theater District, located near Broadway and 42nd Street. Each of these theatres offers a different play or musical to enjoy.

While Broadway shows are always lavish, New York also has a number of "off Broadway" theaters where simpler, often experimental, productions are held. If an off-Broadway production is successful, it may eventually move to a Broadway theatre.

Away from Broadway, the Public Theater holds free productions in Central Park every summer. Further uptown is Lincoln Center, where a mixture of different performing arts can be seen and heard. Twelve different resident companies make up Lincoln Center, including the world-famous

◄ Known as "the house that Ruth built" for baseball star Babe Ruth, Yankee Stadium is still a great sports arena. Here the Yankees play the Detroit Tigers.

The Lost Teams: the Giants and the Dodgers

September 29, 1957, was a sad day for New York baseball fans. On that date, the Brooklyn Dodgers and the New York Giants played their last games. The Brooklyn Dodgers are still fondly remembered as the team that broke the color barrier when African-American Jackie Robinson played for them in 1947. A gifted athlete, Robinson was the first African American to play on a major league baseball team. The Giants, meanwhile, were known for their star player: Willie Mays.

Metropolian Opera, the New York Philharmonic Orchestra, Jazz at Lincoln Center, and the New York City Ballet.

The Garden

While the theaters of Broadway and Lincoln Center have a serious artistic purpose, just about anything can happen in Madison Square Garden. The Garden is a huge indoor arena where sporting events, rock concerts, and even political rallies take

"This is a wonderful city. There is a special fitness in the first syllable of its name, for it is essentially New, and seems likely always to remain..."

—Charles Eliot Norton, historian, 1861.

place. This is where the spectacular "Concert for New York City" was held after the terrorist attacks on the World Trade Center in 2001.

Sporting Life

Sports have always been popular in New York City. Baseball has long been a favorite, and remains so today. This is not surprising, considering that the New York Yankees have won the World Series many times. Yankee Stadium, located in the Bronx, is almost as famous as the team that plays there. Yankee games are always well attended.

Many New Yorkers are also fans of New York City's other baseball team, the Mets. The Mets play their home games at Shea Stadium, in Queens. Regular attendances for Met games is over 35,000.

Apart from baseball, New York is home to a number of distinguished teams, including the New York Knicks in basketball and the Rangers in ice hockey. Both these teams play their home games at Madison Square Garden.

Although the Giants and the Jets are New York's two National Football League teams, both teams play their home games in Giants Stadium in New Jersey. This stadium, which has room for almost 80,000 people, has been home for the Giants since 1976. The Jets have played there since 1984, when the team moved from Shea Stadium in Queens.

Museums and Galleries

Baseball games and Broadway shows can be expensive. New York has several libraries, museums, and art galleries that either are free or charge only a small admission fee.

The American Museum of Natural History, located on Manhattan's Upper West Side just next to Central Park, specializes in "living history." Visitors come to see its fossil collection, dinosaur exhibit, planetarium, and for the 95-foot (29-m) reproduction of a blue whale, suspended from the ceiling.

Meanwhile, on the opposite side of Central Park is the Metropolitan Museum of Art. The "Met" was founded in 1870 and now welcomes over five million visitors every year. These guests flock to see the collection of more than two million paintings and works of art displayed in the two hundred fifty rooms of the museum.

While the Met includes works by many world-famous artists of the more distant past, like Rembrandt and Van Gogh, modern artists have their works displayed at the Museum of Modern Art (MoMA). The museum features works by Jackson Pollock, Picasso, and Andy Warhol.

"New York is what Paris was in the twenties... the center of the art world... It's the greatest place on earth."

—John Lennon, musician, 1975.

▲ *Visitors wander through the main entrance hall of the Metropolitan Museum of Art. The museum has more than two million art objects in its exhibit rooms.*

Another museum that focuses on contemporary artists is the Guggenheim, which has two branches, one far uptown and one downtown. The Guggenheim displays works by Paul Klee and Vasily Kandinsky.

Possibly the most modern museum of all is the Museum of Television and Radio. Since opening in 1976, this museum has sought to preserve important television and radio broadcasts. It holds many special exhibits every year that highlight varied types of programming like animation and foreign television programs.

The New York Public Library

The New York Public Library offers forms of entertainment that people can take home. This huge library system has a total of eighty-five branches in Manhattan, the Bronx, and Staten Island. Best-known, however, is the head-quarters and main research library (below) located in midtown Manhattan. This building features two lion statues guarding its entrance, named Patience and Fortitude.

A Popular Hobby

Shopping is perhaps the New Yorker's most famous and most widespread hobby.

There are several big department stores and hundreds of smaller stores in New York City.

Manhattan Magic

To some extent, the entire island of Manhattan can be described as one big shopping center. Specific areas of the city are famous for particular types of stores. Fifth Avenue, for instance, has long been the home of ritzy clothing and jewelry stores like Tiffany's, Saks Fifth Avenue, and Bergdorf Goodman. Less expensive (and possibly more trendy) clothing can often be found in the many used clothing stores downtown like Andy's Chee-Pees. Times Square, on the other hand, is the center for "tourist trap" shops that sell miniature replicas of the Empire State Building and New York bumper stickers.

Macy's and Bloomingdale's

The Macy's chain has department stores all over the United States, but the flagship store is located at Broadway and West 34th Street in Manhattan. The original Macy's store was actually on 14th Street, but in 1902 it moved to its current location. The spectacular balloons that float down Broadway each year on Thanksgiving morning are the highlight of the Macy's Thanksgiving Day Parade.

A longtime rival of Macy's is Bloomingdale's, on 59th Street and Lexington Avenue. Two brothers, Joseph

Gimbels

At one time, both Macy's and Bloomingdale's had a third competitor: Gimbels. The first Gimbels in New York City, which was located very near where Macy's now stands, was opened in 1910. By the 1980s, after much success, the store was struggling to survive. It closed in 1987.

and Lyman Bloomingdale, started Bloomingdale's in 1872. Their shop quickly became famous for selling fashionable European clothes. Like Macy's, the original Bloomingdale's store was in a different location, in this case on the Upper East Side. The move to 59th Street took place in 1886.

FAO Schwarz

Macy's and Bloomingdale's are fine for clothing, but the best toy shopping can be done at FAO Schwarz. The "FAO" stands for Frederick August Otto Schwarz, who opened his first store in Baltimore, Maryland, and moved to New York

"The city is like poetry; it compresses all life, all races and breeds, into a small island and adds music and the accompaniment of internal engines."

—E.B. White, author, 1949.

in 1870. The toy store is famous for its robot-shaped elevator.

Fresh Air

New Yorkers and tourists can pause for breath in several green spaces. Battery Park is at the southern tip of Manhattan and contains the lovely old Castle Clinton. It is popular at lunchtime with workers from the Wall Street area. Prospect Park in Brooklyn is the location of the Brooklyn Public Library main building (built in the shape of a book), and the Brooklyn Botanical Gardens are within the park itself.

The biggest and best park that New York has to offer, though, is Central Park. Central Park is the green heart of New York City, sitting right in the middle of Manhattan. Opened in 1859, it covers 843 acres (341 hectares) and includes statues, lakes, and playgrounds. Visitors can spend an entire day just walking through Central Park, enjoying its beauty.

Central Park also has a fine zoo, but a much more extensive zoo is outside of Manhattan. At the Bronx Zoo, fantastic exhibits and exotic animals can be found. The most recent addition, the Congo Gorilla Forest, is an enormous replica of an African rain forest and includes almost three hundred animals.

▼ *Horse-drawn Hansom cabs make riders feel they are a part of the city's past.*

Looking Forward

There seems to be more of everything in New York City. This includes good things—like food, entertainment, and art—and bad things like traffic, noise, and pollution. It can be an intimidating city. It is not a good place to live if you dislike crowds. Living in New York City can be very expensive as well.

But more often than not, New York's biggest problem is trying to overcome the impressions that people who don't live there have of it. This is not just damaging to New York's public image, but also—more importantly—to its economy.

Crime

In many ways, New York City is as famous for its crime as for anything else. This may be due, in part, to the fact that New York City is such a media center. Crimes that are also common in other major cities receive worldwide exposure in New York newspapers and magazines. Many television shows and movies have depicted New York as a violent, dangerous city. Fear of New York crime has meant lost business and fewer tourists.

However, New York is not the most violent city in the United States. According to statistics, it is not even among the

◄ *Times Square is always thronging with people and excitement, but especially on New Year's Eve, when a giant ball drops to signal the start of the next year.*

top twenty-five most violent cities in the country.

Over the years, public officials have fought against the stereotype of New York City crime. Mayor Rudolph Giuliani became famous for fighting New York crime with the assistance of the seventy-six precincts of the New York Police Department. At various times, crime rates have fallen, but crime is a problem that is never completely beaten.

Changes in Store

The population of New York continues to grow. For the people who have come from other countries, New York City represents freedom and the promise of a better life. For the people who move there from other parts of America, New York City represents buzz and adventure.

For many people, New York City represents change. New York restaurants open and close in an instant. Stores come and go. People constantly switch jobs and apartments.

New Yorkers are not always happy about this constant change. The renovation of

"…once you have lived in New York and it has become your home, no place else is good enough."

—John Steinbeck, author, 1943.

The Big Apple

New York City has many nicknames. The most well known, however, is a term that was originally coined by jazz musicians in the 1930s. Back then, musicians referred to any town or city as an "apple." New York, though, was special. New York was—in their estimation—"The Big Apple," the biggest and most exciting city of all.

Times Square during the mid-1990s, for instance, was met by many with scorn.

Currently, a committee is working to bring the 2012 Olympic Games to New York City. Likewise, plans are being discussed to revitalize the area of lower Manhattan where the World Trade Center once stood. Inventive ways are being found to put the old shipping docks to good use. The enormous sports complex built on the Chelsea Piers is a good example. It takes up four piers on the Hudson River and is outfitted with skating rinks, basketball courts, rock climbing walls, and more.

Four Hundred Years On

It has been almost four hundred years since the Dutch founded the town that eventually became New York City. New York still shows no signs of slowing down, and it is a city that is never completely finished.

Time Line

9,000 B.C. Native Americans begin to settle in the New York area.

A.D. 1609 English explorer Henry Hudson arrives in the New York area.

1624 New Amsterdam, the first Dutch colony in the area, is established.

1664 New Amsterdam is taken by the British and renamed New York.

1732 The first play is performed in New York City.

1775 War breaks out between the American colonists and the British.

1776 The Declaration of Independence is adopted.

1783 The British leave New York.

1785 New York is named the temporary capital of the United States of America.

1789 George Washington is sworn in as the first U.S. president in New York.

1790 The U.S. capital changes location to Philadelphia, Pennsylvania.

1792 The New York Stock Exchange is founded.

1825 The Erie Canal is opened.

1827 New York state outlaws slavery.

1853 New York City begins free public education.

1859 Central Park opens.

1870 The Metropolitan Museum of Art is founded.

1871 The "el" trains start operating.

1886 The Statue of Liberty is given to the United States by France.

1892 Ellis Island opens.

1898 The five boroughs are consolidated into the City of Greater New York.

1902 The Flatiron Building is completed.

1904 The city's first subway line opens.

1905 The Staten Island Ferry begins operation.

1921 The National Origins Act restricts immigration.

1924 The Johnson-Reed Act further restricts immigration.

1929 The Wall Street Crash occurs; the Great Depression starts.

1930 The Chrysler Building is completed.

1931 The Empire State Building is completed.

1939 The World's Fair begins in Queens.

1957 New York City loses two baseball teams, the Dodgers and the Giants.

1964 The World's Fair is held again in Queens.

1965 Immigration quotas are significantly relaxed.

1973 The World Trade Center is completed.

1987 Another Wall Street crash signals the start of a recession.

2001 The World Trade Center twin towers are destroyed by terrorists.

Glossary

Algonquin a North American Indian group.

boroughs towns that make up a larger city.

botanical gardens large gardens with many specimens of different plants.

canal an artificial waterway used for shipping and navigation.

capital the center of government for a nation or state.

consensus agreement among different people or groups.

containerization a method of shipping that involves packing goods in large containers.

copyrighting legally protecting a document or image so that permission is required to reproduce it.

depression a period of economic slump.

draft compulsory enlistment in the military.

Episcopal a Protestant Christian church that broke away from the Church of England after the American Revolution.

ethnic of a particular race or cultural group.

Gaelic language of the Celts, a people who lived in Ireland in ancient times.

gold standard monetary system in which the basic unit of currency has the same value as a specific amount of gold.

Hispanics people of Latin-American descent.

immigration the process of moving from one country to another to live.

Latinos people of Latin-American descent.

legislation laws and lawmaking.

media newspapers, radio, television; the different means of transmitting information.

naturalization the process of becoming an American citizen.

quota (immigrant) the number of immigrants from a particular country that are allowed to enter the new country.

radically extremely.

settlement a small town or village.

stock small part of ownership of a company.

stock market place where stock can be bought and sold.

suspension bridge a kind of bridge in which the roadway is suspended by cables that hang from large towers.

traders dealers; people who sell or exchange particular goods.

Further Information

Books

Anderson, Dale. *Arriving at Ellis Island (Landmark Events in American History).* World Almanac Library, 2002.

Anderson, Dale. *The Attacks on September 11, 2001 (Landmark Events in American History).* World Almanac Library, 2003.

Kent, Deborah. *New York City (Cities of the World).* Children's Press, 1996.

Lalley, Patrick. *9.11.01 – Terrorists Attack the U.S.* Raintree Steck-Vaughn Publishers, 2002.

Tagliaferro, Linda. *Destination New York. (Port Cities of North America).* Lerner Publications Company, 1998.

Web sites

http://www.nyc.gov
The official New York City government web site.

http://www.ny.com/
Guide to history, local news, weather, and events in New York City.

http://www.ellisisland.com/
Ellis Island Immigration Museum.

http://www.amnh.org/
American Museum of Natural History.

http://www.nypl.org/
New York Public Library.

http://www.childnet/nyckids.htm/
Web site for kids in New York City.

http://wcs.org/home/zoos/bronxzoo/
Web page of the Wildlife Conservation Society and the Bronx Zoo.

http://www.greatgridlock.net/NYC/nycfront.html
New York City Skyscrapers.

http://www.nytimes.com/
Home page for the New York Times.

Index

DATE DUE

DATE DUE	
JUN 2 3 2004	
OCT 1 9 2004	
FEB 1 9 2005	
APR 0 4 2005	
MAY 1 8 2005	
OCT 2 4 2005	
NOV 1 6 2005	